CONFESSIONS OF MURDER

CONFESSIONS OF MURDER

EXPOSING THE FALSE CONFESSIONS CREATED FROM THE MR. BIG STINGS

ALAN R. WARREN

COPYRIGHT

CONFESSIONS OF MURDER: Exposing the False Confessions
Created from Mr. Big Stings
Written by Alan R. Warren

Published in Canada

Copyright @ 2020 by Alan R. Warren

All rights reserved. No part of this book may be reproduced, scanned, or distributed in any printed or electronic form without permission of the author. The unauthorized reproduction of a copyrighted work is illegal. Criminal copyright infringement, including infringement without monetary gain, is investigated by the FBI and is punishable by fines and federal imprisonment. Please do not participate in or encourage privacy of copyrighted materials in violation of the author's rights. Purchase only authorized editions.

This is a work of nonfiction. No names have been changed, no characters invented, no events fabricated.

Cover design, formatting and layout by Evening Sky Publishing Services

BOOK DESCRIPTION

It started with a frantic call for help from Sebastian Burns and Atif Rafay, when the two boys arrived home at just after 2 a.m. on July 13, 1994 and found Rafay's family brutally beaten to death in their Bellevue, Washington, home. Who would kill this well-liked family in such a horrific way? Police had no physical evidence and no witnesses; the case was a dead end! It was time to bring in Mr. Big!

Mr. Big is a covert investigation where undercover detectives create a fictitious criminal gang and seduce their suspects into joining them in their criminal activities, and police would soon gain their suspects' confidence and elicit a confession from them.

Burns and Rafay would eventually confess on tape to undercover detectives and be convicted of the three murders of Rafay's family. In the last 25 years, the RCMP (Royal Canadian Mounted Police) have run more than 350 Mr. Big operations on suspects of crimes where there was no evidence found and have had a 95% success rate in prosecution.

It was in July 2014 when the Supreme Court of Canada ruled unanimously that confessions arising from the Mr. Big operations would be considered presumptively inadmissible on another case against Nelson Hart. The Mr. Big Sting in the Hart case was said to have overwhelming inducements, veiled threats of violence, and intimidation and considered an abuse of process by the police.

So now what will happen to the hundreds of other cases that have been tried by this unreliable procedure in which the Mr. Big coerced confession was the only evidence used to convict the suspect? This book will cover the cases that have now been brought back into court on appeals based on the Mr. Big operation, and will explain the outcomes.

CONTENTS

Preface — ix
Introduction — xi

1. Burns And Rafay Case — 1
2. The Nelson Hart Case — 15
3. Amanda Cook Murder Case — 21
4. Kyle Unger Case — 25
5. Alan Smith 2009 — 31
6. Daniel Morcombe Murder — 39
7. Operation Ezdell — 45
8. Klaus Family Murder — 51
9. Gary Johnston Surrey — 57
10. Project Kolumbo — 63
11. Derek Kembel Murder Case — 69
12. Andrew Rose — 75
13. Innocence Project — 83
14. Project Souvenir — 91
    Epilogue — 97

Acknowledgments — 99
About the Author — 101
Also by Alan R. Warren — 103
References — 107

PREFACE

Beverly Smith was a 22-year-old new mother who was shot to death in her kitchen while her infant daughter watched on a chilly winter night in 1974. Her neighbor at the time, Alan Smith, confessed to the crime and was convicted of first-degree murder and sent to prison for life.

On August 4, 2002, Nelson Hart took his 3-year-old twin daughters to a quiet beach near Gander, Newfoundland, where both girls drowned. Hart, being unable to swim, couldn't save them. Three years later, Hart confessed to murdering his daughters, and on March 28, 2007, Hart was convicted of first-degree murder and sentenced to life.

These cases seem cut and dry, right? Wrong!

In both of the previous cases the police used an undercover operation that has become known as the Mr. Big Sting. This is a covert investigation procedure used by undercover detectives to get a confession from a suspect in a case where they don't have enough evidence to convict.

The plan is to create a fictitious gang that enlist the

help of the suspect in a succession of criminal acts to a point where they have a friendship, and soon the suspect openly talks about previous criminal accomplishments. So, when the suspect confesses a crime, it is videotaped; they are arrested and charged with the crime. There have been over 500 current convictions by using this method.

In 2012, the Supreme Court of Newfoundland overturned Hart's conviction, questioning the reliability of his confession to undercover officers posing as members of the mob. The Crown then appealed this to the Supreme Court of Canada.

Then in 2014, the Supreme Court of Canada ruled that Hart's confession during the sting operation cannot be used against him and should be excluded. Following this, the Alan Smith case was also reversed on the same grounds. So, it would appear that Canada now has over 500 cases where the person charged has been tried, convicted and sentenced by using this police technique.

Now before us will be the steady stream of appeals on all cases that have used any evidence that was obtained by the Mr. Big Sting operation, and even with this obstacle ahead of the justice system, the RCMP (Royal Canadian Mounted Police) are still planning on using this method to gather evidence on all open cases that they deem necessary.

This type of policing is not legally allowed in the United States or the United Kingdom as both countries have deemed it entrapment. In this book, I plan to detail the Mr. Big operation, as well as what it looks like from the people that it gets used on, as well as some of the unanswered questions that we are left with.

INTRODUCTION

The Mr. Big, or also known as the Canadian Technique, is a covert investigation procedure that is used by the RCMP in Canada. This is where undercover police try to get a confession from suspects in murder cases, usually cold cases.

It all starts with the police creating a fictitious criminal organization and trying to get the suspects of a murder case to join their group. Over a period, they build a relationship and gain trust with the suspects by using them in a series of criminal acts such as credit card scams, stealing cars or improperly selling guns.

It was in 1901 when Donald Todd was convicted for a murder in Winnipeg after a Mr. Big operation. Even though the court noted that the means employed to obtain the confession were contemptible, they convicted him.

The Mr. Big technique then was developed by the RCMP in the early 1990s and has been used in more than 350 cases across Canada. The RCMP claimed that they have a 75 percent cleared rate on the cases that they have taken on in this technique, and have a 95 percent conviction rate.

In more detail, in a typical Mr. Big sting, the first thing that the undercover police usually do is place the suspect under 24-hour surveillance for weeks or even months, looking to find out the habits and things that they did daily. With this information, police would create a scenario where they could meet the suspect by accident. In these meetings, the undercover officer would ask for help in some way or perhaps a small favor from the suspect. The operative would then offer to buy the suspect's dinner or even offer employment.

From there it begins; the suspect would now be asked to do small jobs for the undercover police, such as count money or make some deliveries, and would be paid exceptionally well for doing the job. The tasks then start to be more challenging and often to where they start to feel more important to the Mr. Big group.

This now leads the suspects to be introduced to the leader of the Mr. Big group, or criminal group's boss. It is there that the pressure is applied to try and get the suspects to confess or brag about the crimes that they have committed previously to joining the Mr. Big gang.

The undercover operation usually employs up to fifty operatives as to help make the Mr. Big group look legitimate as well as apply pressures to the suspect to feel safe to talk about crimes of their past.

Shortly after the undercover police learn of crimes committed by the suspects, their operative, posing as the gang leader, would approach the suspect and tell them of some information they had learned. It would be information pertaining to the suspect's previous crimes, such as he heard that the police were about to make an arrest for the crime.

Mr. Big would then offer to help with this problem by perhaps helping to fix the criminal situation in which the suspect had been involved by several different methods. One such method could be that Mr. Big has an insider working for the police that could get rid of the evidence that's on file for the crime.

Another way that the Mr. Big sting could be used is telling the suspect that for them to go further into the gang, they would need to give up some incriminating evidence about themselves. This would act as collateral or some sort of insurance that shows the Mr. Big gang loyalty.

These meetings are always recorded so that they have a copy of the confessions for possible trial in the future. Once enough information is recorded to prosecute the suspect, usually an arrest is made.

RCMP claim that they only use the Mr. Big technique on cold cases where there just isn't enough evidence to prove the case.

The police stick with this technique as it has been used to secure convictions in hundreds of cases since it started just over twenty years ago, whereas false confessions are few and considered worth the risk.

Most of the criticism of the Mr. Big technique comes from the program being very invasive into the suspects' lives. The RCMP essentially infiltrate the target's life and can even change their future life. The operation also involves the abuse of trust in personal relationships.

The other major issue is that the complete records of the sting are not available to the public or even defense lawyers. Most of the scenarios brought forward in the case are documented in a retrospective way by the operatives, which only allows evidence which is needed for the conviction.

So far it all sounds great, right? On the surface it seems like a completely sound way to get the evidence needed to catch a serious bad guy for a crime such as murder, but there's a darker side to the so-called Mr. Big technique that has been used in Canada now for over twenty years. The Rafay and Burns case made everyone aware of how this operation is not used or legally allowed to be used in both the United Kingdom or the United States. Why is this? After all, we are so socially related to both countries, what is it about the sting that isn't allowed? One word, entrapment.

BURNS AND RAFAY CASE

"The life of the dead is placed in the memory of the living" – Marcus Tullius Cicero

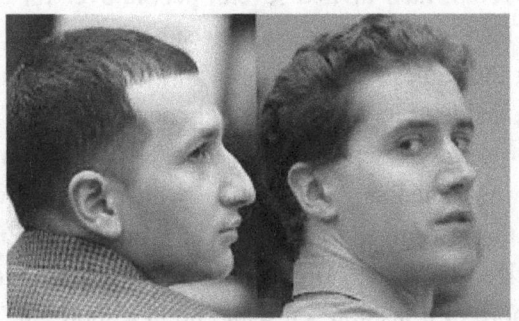

Atif Rafay and Sebastian Burns

When Sebastian Burns met Atif Rafay in high school, there was an instant friendship, almost as if he knew Atif his whole life. The two boys were very intelligent and well read, which would often lead to all-night discussions about life and philosophy.

Burns was very popular amongst his classmates at school. He was good looking, friendly, and very helpful to all of those around him. He was raised in the West Vancouver community, which was an upper middle-class area, with very little crime. His parents were of British descent and led a disciplined life with lots of structure. There would never be a time where Sebastian would leave his room a mess or would use swear words to anybody that visited their home.

Sebastian took part in lots of activities in school, including acting and singing in the drama department. Burns starred in the 1929 British play called "Rope" which would come to haunt him later in life. It happened to be a story of two young University students that killed one of their classmates, put him in a chest in their first-floor sitting room, then invited several people over for a buffet party. They wanted to prove their superior intelligence by having their guests dine on top of the chest with the body hidden inside of it, without anybody noticing.

Burns was very physically active, too, and belonged to the Royal Canadian Air Cadets in which he once won an award that was given to him by Prince Edward of England. For Atif to be around Burns, he would learn how to dress with more of a fashion sense and be in a spotlight, always having Burns by his side.

Rafay had just gotten into and attended his first year at Cornell University, and though he was struggling with the classes, he loved the challenge that was presented by the top-ranked college known for its Law and Management Departments.

Atif's father, Tariq Rafay, was a structural engineer who had worked on buildings around the world. Sultana, Atif's mother, had her doctorate in nutrition and devoted her life to raising Basma, her autistic daughter, and running the household. The family had recently moved to Bellevue, Washington, from Vancouver B.C., Canada, and Atif and Sebastian decided to spend a couple of weeks there during their summer break.

It was around 2 a.m. on July 14, 1994, when the call came into the 911 center from Sebastian Burns's where he was reporting a break-in at the Rafay house. They waited outside until the police showed up. Upon entering the home, police found Tariq Rafay, Atif's father, still lying in his bed face up. He had been beaten so badly that his facial features were unrecognizable, and his teeth were scattered around the bedroom.

Atif's mother was found in the basement, beaten to death as well, and his sister Basma was lying close by, but still alive. They rushed her to the hospital where she died a few hours later.

Police took Sebastian and Atif to the station and questioned them about what had happened that night. When asked where they had been that evening, the boys provided a full account. At 8:30 p.m., they drove to a restaurant for a bite to eat. Then they went to a 9:50 p.m. showing of *The Lion King*. After the movie, they stopped for a bite to eat and left the waitress a $6 tip on a $9 tab.

"Everywhere they went, the people who had contact with them remembered them,"

---

says Konat. But something else troubled police. The police then examined Burns and Rafay for traces of blood, where they found nothing.

On the night of the murder, Bellevue police, after questioning the two young men, didn't arrest them. Instead, they put them up in a hotel with pagers and contact information and told them to get some sleep.

How could Sebastian and Atif provide so much detail about where they had been that evening, but not recall key moments at the murder scene? Cops became even more suspicious when Sebastian and Atif were spotted at a local video store renting a movie the night after the murders.

So, the police pressed the boys further on what happened in the Rafay house. They wanted to know why Atif didn't help his dying sister, even though he heard her through the bedroom door. Three days after the murders, relatives of the Rafays gathered in Bellevue to bury the victims. But the only surviving member of the immediate family, Atif, was nowhere to be found. When Atif Rafay missed his family's memorial at a Northgate mosque and he was video-taped laughing, all hell broke loose. Atif Rafay claims he wasn't informed of the memorial.

Burns and Rafay were on a bus headed across the border to Canada to go live with Burns's family in Vancouver; the boys were out of reach of Bellevue detectives and an investigation that targeted them for the murders of the Rafay family.

Their sudden bus trip across the border only raised more suspicion, even though both boys were Canadian citizens. In fact, a representative from the Canadian consulate informed the Bellevue police of their trip in advance. Detective Thompson's gut told him that the boys were guilty, but he just didn't have the evidence to prove it. Investigators kept combing the house.

They found no forced entry. However, when they used luminol throughout the house, it showed an enormous amount of blood on the shower walls. The killer had used the shower before leaving. Could that be the reason why the boys, who discovered the bodies, didn't have a trace of blood on their hair, their hands, or anywhere on their bodies?

Even without physical evidence, detectives were determined. They began to build a case against the boys based on their odd behavior following the murders. "They cooperated," says Thompson. "They did everything that was asked of them. However, when they did things, they had this air or this attitude about doing it."

They homed in on the boys' demeanor at the crime scene and questioned why they sat in front of the house if they believed an intruder might still be there. Police also couldn't make sense of why Atif would notice that his Disc-man and VCR were missing.

Sebastian's family and friends rallied around him and Atif. "I believe him to be totally innocent, as is Atif. And they have been damned," says Sebastian's father, Dave Burns. On the advice of a lawyer, the boys decided to stop cooperating with Bellevue authorities.

Thompson kept digging into the boys' past and found what he thought was a disturbing clue. He discovered that Sebastian was in a high school play called *Rope*, about two kids who commit the perfect murder. Detectives believed the fictional murder story inspired the real-life crime, and even more chilling, the weapon used was the same, a baseball bat. "That's just a huge coincidence, and it's nothing more than that," says Dave Burns. "I think Sebastian was actually mortified when he realized that he was a suspect in the baseball-bat killings of the Rafays, because he said,

---

> "Cripes, what's gonna happen when they find out about the play?"

As the investigation continued, the boys were living well in Vancouver with some of the money Atif inherited from his parents' estate. They bought a convertible and rented an apartment along with another high school pal, Jimmy Miyoshi. Behind drawn curtains, they hid from the media who were constantly in pursuit of them and their story. But what they didn't realize was that they were now the targets of the RCMP.

On April 10, 1995, RCMP investigators intercepted a phone message confirming a salon appointment with Sebastian. By then, Sebastian and Atif were Canada's most famous teenage murder suspects. But the boys had a plan to make their fortune and live out a lifelong dream.

They started work on their very own screenplay about two best friends accused of murdering a family. They called the screenplay, *The Great Despisers*. But they had no idea the real-life plot line was about to take an astonishing turn. That simple message from a local hair salon was the moment the RCMP was waiting for.

As Sebastian left the salon, a stranger approached him, asking for a ride to his hotel. The stranger then took Sebastian to a bar and bought him a drink for his trouble. Sebastian told this stranger that he and his buddies had written a screenplay. Sebastian said he didn't have a job and needed financing.

The stranger said he knew someone who could help.

"Ultimately, the goal was to get Sebastian to meet with the next guy up the chain,"

---

says Konat. "And it worked perfectly." Sebastian thought he was about to meet a connected businessman. But he met with Sergeant Haslett of the RCMP, working undercover.

The RCMP, which spent months preparing to manipulate their target, posed as professional mobsters and set up their first meeting with Sebastian in a strip club. The crime boss told Sebastian he had cash to invest in his screenplay, but Sebastian would have to earn it.

Sebastian had no idea, however, that he was being offered work in a make-believe world of crime. Jobs were also promised to Atif and Miyoshi. Sebastian's first assignment was to transport a stolen car for the crime boss for $200.

Then Sebastian and Jimmy Miyoshi went from one bank to another laundering money. For a day's work, they were paid $2,000 cash. Months went by, and the undercover operators took Sebastian to posh hotels trying to build trust and draw him out.

The mobsters slowly brought up the topic of the investigation in Bellevue, and Haslett tried to draw Sebastian out by telling him he already knew what happened. Sebastian didn't admit guilt, but he confided in the mobsters that if the police did find something to tie him to the crime, he might want them to destroy it. And he had a very practical theory.

As one of the best-known murder suspects in Canada, Sebastian was confident that his movie would make millions if he was suddenly proven innocent. So, the businessmen raised the stakes and told Sebastian that the Bellevue police had physical evidence tying him to the crime. And to make it real, Haslett shows Sebastian a phoney memo on Bellevue Police letterhead detailing the evidence linking Sebastian to the murders. The mobsters offer to destroy the so-called evidence, but they need Sebastian to tell them exactly what happened in the Rafay house the night of the murders.

Finally, on July 18, 1995, one year after the murders, Sebastian meets Haslett at the Ocean Point Resort, and the cameras are rolling. Konat says,

> "He walks into this hotel room and takes off his shoes. He stretches out on a love seat, and it's at that point he lets his guard down. And the dirty little secret that he's been protecting for the last 12 or 13 months starts to unravel on video for the whole wide world to see."

It had taken three months of undercover work to get to this moment. The next day, Sebastian brought Atif to the crime boss to tell his story, which was recorded on an undercover tape. It was all the police needed to hear.

In a series of secretly videotaped encounters at hotel rooms from Whistler to Victoria, the young men admitted to killing the Rafay family. Canada eventually agreed to deport the pair but only after securing a guarantee that the young men would not face the death penalty.

The videotaped interviews they got with the giggling, boasting Canadian teens formed the backbone of the U.S. prosecution. Outside the courtroom, prosecutor James Konat said the guilty verdicts are a vindication of the RCMP methods and the proper result for a stomach-turning crime. The prosecution has said the family was killed to get insurance money. Tariq Rafay, his wife Sultana and their 20-year-old autistic daughter, Basma, were found beaten to death with baseball bats in their suburban Seattle home in July 1994.

Sebastian Burns narrowed his eyes and glared at jury members who pronounced him guilty on three first-degree murder counts. Beside him, his partner in crime, Atif Rafay, whose family the pair slaughtered on a July night 10 years ago, closed his eyes and shook his head in disbelief after he, too, was found guilty.

As the sheriffs approached to handcuff the men, Mr. Burns turned and faced his stricken family. He shrugged and rolled his eyes while his sister reached her arms toward him. The detached reaction to the sobering verdicts was in keeping with the men's demeanor throughout the six-month trial.

Each day, they sat in court quietly conferring with their lawyers and smiling and chatting with one another. Their defense was that they were set up by police. They said they lied to the undercover officers because they believed they were criminals and were afraid of them. Mr. Burns said he believed one would shoot him. Prosecutors said this bravado was the boys' hallmark characteristic. But their hubris and arrogance helped seal their fate.

Outside court, Mr. Konat said he thought jury members came to "despise" the defendants. The prosecutor also said Mr. Burns's decision to testify backfired. On the witness stand earlier this month, he came off as arrogant and unfeeling and his explanation for why he would have given a false confession didn't ring true.

Mr. Burns's parents and sister rushed from the courthouse as soon the court was adjourned, refusing to talk to reporters.

American authorities consider the "Mr. Big" sting entrapment. Police in the United States are not allowed to issue threats or offer suspected criminals promises, money or alcohol in exchange for confessions. And no U.S. court considers these types of confessions admissible except in the case of two young Canadian men charged with committing murder in Bellevue, Washington, Sebastian Burns and Atif Rafay.

Both Burns and Rafay, who were now 28 years old, would be sentenced to spend the rest of their lives in an American prison with no chance of parole. It was apparent that Sebastian Burns was playing to whoever would watch him. During the sentencing hearing in a Seattle courtroom, Burns would direct his comments to the cameras which were permitted in the U.S. courtrooms. He suggested that the Washington police didn't investigate any other suspects and even that extremist Muslims might have killed Rafay's family.

Burns knew what cards to play in the audience of Americans as both police falsely imprisoning innocent people and the terrorist attacks that were already on their minds daily. "I think any objective professional, any objective lay person, would conclude that we were defending ourselves in this trial with both arms tied behind our back," Burns said with anger in his eyes.

Judge Mertel asked Burns to wrap up his statement, then sentenced him to life without parole and said,

---

"Mr. Burns, you are not immoral, you are amoral. You have no moral rudder."

This was the case that not only affected the victims' families and friends, but would have an enormous impact on the legal system of not just the United States but Canada as well. The case became mired in notoriety over police tactics and the fight to have these boys extradited to the United States to stand trial for the murders.

Since the conviction, Sebastian Burns has exhausted all his appeals and Atif Rafay still has one last appeal left.

The current defense thinks that the Mr. Big operation was highly coercive and do not think it should have been allowed in a U.S. court, and there should also be consideration of their age, juveniles given life without parole in the U.S., and giving a lot of thought about the brain of a juvenile and how they respond differently to the world than an adult would.

But the King County Prosecutor's Office feels otherwise. In a statement released September 20, Daniel T. Satterberg's office said the two episodes, totaling 90 minutes,

> "do not present a full or fair account of the crime, the defendants' confessions, or the evidence presented at the six-month trial. Although the focus of the episodes is on the allegedly false confessions, most of the confessions (which were recorded on audio and videotape) are neither played nor described. Moreover, the show does not even mention that Burns testified at trial and the jury was able to directly evaluate his claim that he did not commit the murders. Evidence that is contrary to the false confession claim is simply omitted from the program."

The prosecutor's office says that not only was evidence omitted but Burns sought out the undercover officers, and

> "repeatedly expressed his willingness to engage in a variety of criminal acts, which he believed he was committing on behalf of a criminal organization."

In addition, Atif Rafay and Burns's friend Jimmy

Miyoshi, who testified at their trial against them, admitted that he knew of their plans to commit the murders and that the motive was financial. Loudenberg said she has the entire interrogation of Miyoshi and said what was left out of the prosecutor's office's statement was the RCMP's threat against Myoshi with 99 years in prison and even a suggestion of the death penalty if he didn't give evidence against his friends.

THE NELSON HART CASE

"The trust of the innocent is the liar's most useful tool." – Stephen King

---

| Nelson Hart on Trial

It was ten years after the murders of the Rafay family in Bellevue, Washington, that the Mr. Big Technique came under fire by the courts. The case was against Nelson Hart who was charged in June of 2005 for the murders of his twin 3-year-old daughters, who died because of drowning on August 4, 2002.

Hart claimed that he had taken his girls, Krista and Karen, to the wharf at Little Harbour, when Krista fell off the wharf, and Hart, who was unable to swim, got scared and ran for help. Hart drove to his home where he got his wife, and they returned to the wharf. By the time they got there, both daughters were in the water now; Krista was dead, but Karen was still alive, so they rushed her to the hospital, where she died within a few hours.

It was later the same year in October when the Mr. Big operation began on Nelson Hart. The Mr. Big surveillance showed that Hart went everywhere with his wife as he had very few friends. Hart had several seizures on a regular basis, which began in the late 1990s when he was involved in a car crash. This was probably one of the main reasons that he was so isolated from other people.

First contact between Hart and the Mr. Big sting was when one of the operatives had offered to pay Hart some money to help find somebody. After that, Hart was asked to make some deliveries on a regular basis and paid very well. A friendship then developed with the operatives.

The illegal activities continued to get more frequent and of a more serious nature. Hart soon brought his wife into his new-found jobs. They began to deal in fake credit cards, passports and even counterfeit casino chips. With large payoffs and luxurious trips around the country, Hart wanted to become a full-time member of the Mr. Big gang.

It was in spring of 2003 when Hart finally met the Boss of his new-found gang. The boss told Hart that there were things that came up in Hart's past that he didn't like. The boss wanted to know about Hart's daughters' deaths, the real story, as he didn't believe the story that Hart had told the police.

Hart felt under extreme pressure, so he confessed to pushing both girls off the wharf. Hart then went to the crime scene with a couple of operatives from the Mr. Big gang and re-enacted the event that had happened with his daughters. The event was videotaped as the gang had wanted some collateral on Hart.

This tape was later used by the prosecution in a trial on March 2007, where a jury ended up convicting Hart of two counts of first-degree murder.

In 2012, Hart appealed his conviction and won a 2-1 split decision in the Court of Appeal who ordered a new trial. Chief Justice Green's statement said,

---

> "Hart was in control of the state in a manner that was equivalent in degree to detention. It was not reasonable to expect that he would have any reason, or take any opportunity, to leave the organization. That meant he had to subscribe to the culture of the organization and to ensure that he continued to receive the approbation of Mr. Big. Although he obviously wanted to maintain that he had an innocent explanation for the deaths of his daughters, he eventually succumbed when it became clear that Mr. Big would accept no other answer than one which accepted his proposition that he was responsible for their murder. For Mr. Hart in the circumstances in which he found himself there was very little downside to telling Mr. Big what he wanted to hear. Since he

> believed the operatives were not police and he had been assured that any information he gave would be kept from authorities. On the other hand, in his mind, Mr. Hart had a great deal to lose if he did not accede to the required admission."

The Appeal Court decided that Hart's Section 7 Charter protections had been breached. The Crown appealed this decision to the Supreme Court of Canada, whose decision was released on July 31, 2014. Writing for a unanimous majority, Justice Moldaver declared,

> "The confessions arising from Mr. Big operations would henceforth be considered presumptively inadmissible, subject to a two-pronged admissibility analysis."

The Supreme Court also alerted trial judges to the possible dangers of abuse of process which might take place during Mr. Big stings, and of the need for scrutiny during the trials. An abuse of process has occurred when police overcome the will of the accused and coerce a confession, as was said to have taken place in *R. v. Hart*.

Overwhelming inducements, veiled threats of violence, and intimidation are examples of conduct that could be considered an abuse of process by police. Now we must ask the question, "Would the decision on the Hart case have any effect on the current murder conviction of Sebastian Burns and Atif Rafay?"

The ruling clarifies for the first time whether the existing legal framework adequately protects the rights of individuals whose confessions were obtained through this technique, and whether these confessions should be admissible in court.

The Supreme Court said that the Mr. Big technique has proven to be an effective investigative tool, but it also comes "with a price."

The strategy, according to the Supreme Court, poses three distinct dangers:

1. **Reliability:** It raises the specter of "unreliable confessions" that have been responsible for wrongful convictions — "a fact," the Supreme Court said, it "cannot ignore."
2. **Prejudice**: The confessions come with evidence that shows the accused took part in "simulated crimes." The Supreme Court said, "this evidence sullies the accused's character and, in doing so, carries with it the risk of prejudice."
3. **Potential for police misconduct:** The stings "run the risk of becoming abusive," the Supreme Court said. "Thought must be given to the kinds of police tactics we, as a society, are prepared to condone in pursuit of the truth."

To ensure trial judges have the tools to address all three issues, Moldaver suggests taking a two-pronged approach that "strikes the best balance between guarding against the dangers posed by Mr. Big operations, while ensuring the police have the tools they need to investigate serious crime."

Moldaver said trial judges may want to start by determining whether there has been an abuse of the process. If there was police misconduct, then there is no need to determine whether the value of the confession outweighs its prejudicial effect.

If the defense cannot establish abuse, the onus is on the Crown to establish that, on balance, the confessions are more reliable than they are prejudicial to the accused. Police have lost a 'strong technique'.

3

AMANDA COOK MURDER CASE

> *"Mistakes are always forgivable, if one has the courage to admit them."* – Bruce Lee

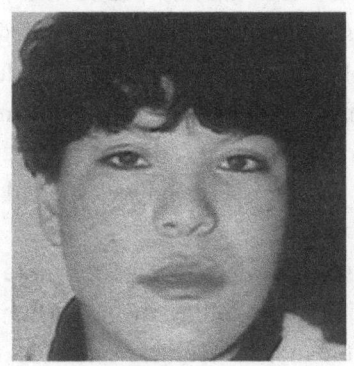

Amanda Cook

It was on July 23, 1996, that 14-year-old Amanda Cook, along with her father, brother, and cousin, went to the Harvest Fair Festival held in Rossburn, Manitoba. They lived at the Waywayseecappo First Nations reservation, which was only about 15 minutes from the fair.

As soon as they arrived at the fair, her father gave the three kids some money and told them to behave, and then he went to the bleachers to watch the races throughout the day. Amanda kept coming interrupting her father in the bleachers to ask him for some more money. The last time he saw her was at about 6:30 to 7 p.m. that night.

When the father tried to round up the kids to go home, he was not able to find Amanda. Soon the police arrived, and a search began, but she was not to be found that night. Four days later, July 17, 1996, the body of Amanda Cook was found partially clothed in the bush only minutes away from where the fair was held.

An autopsy was later performed where it was determined that Amanda had died from multiple blows to the head. It took several months before the police arrested Clayton George Mentuck for the second-degree murder of Amanda Cook. It was learned that Mentuck was seen talking to Amanda just before she went missing. Suspicions grew when Mentuck left the reservation just days after Amanda went missing and was spotted hitchhiking to Vancouver.

Mentuck then wrote a confession note to Amanda's parents after his arrest telling them that he had murdered Amanda. In the note, Mentuck said that he had killed Amanda by dropping a large rock onto her head.

The Crown tried Mentuck three times; the first trial in 1996 ended in a stay, after it was found that the tape of Mentuck confessing to the murder had been altered and 17 minutes of the tape were missing.

The second trial in September 1998, ended with a hung jury, as the jury wasn't fully convinced by the prosecution's main witness, who testified that Mentuck had told him about how he had murdered Amanda Cook while they were in prison together for another minor crime.

In the third trial in 2000, the judge found him not guilty of the second-degree murder. The confession note that Mentuck had written was deemed inadmissible in court; therefore, the police gave it to Amanda's parents. Mentuck had denied that he was involved in the killing, and even after he confessed, he wrote a note saying that his confession was untrue and that he was confused.

It was the court's opinion that during the undercover operation, the police had involved Mentuck in so many criminal acts, that they enticed him to confess to the killing.

Mary, Amanda's mother, now says, "I still have it" (the confession note). "I just keep it. I never showed it to nobody. I just keep it hidden with the rest of the papers I have with everything. "

Before this case, the Canadian public had never heard about the tactics used by our national police. But the *Winnipeg Free Press* fought all the way to the Supreme Court for the right to report the details of the RCMP investigation that led Mentuck to falsely confess to murder.

Ultimately the lawsuit filed by the Free Press had broader implications than just one case. It was the turning point for journalists to start writing and talking about an undercover operation in which the police pretend to be criminals to coerce confessions.

It is an operation that targets dozens of suspects each year, but the RCMP have been extremely secretive about

24 | CONFESSIONS OF MURDER

the numbers surrounding "Mr. Big," such as, how much does it cost the taxpayer, exactly how many stings are done each year, what is their success rate and how is that success rate defined?

4

KYLE UNGER CASE

Another Manitoba man convicted of murder thanks to a "Mr. Big sting" is currently free on bail after 14 years in jail, thanks to a DNA review. Kyle Unger maintains his 1991 murder confession is false.

It was on June 22, 1990, that then nineteen-year-old Kyle Unger was at a rock concert with his friend, John Beckett, at a nearby ski resort.

At the same concert was Timothy Houlahan, 17, who appeared to be with Brigette Grenier, 16, as they were on the concert floor dancing, kissing, and groping each other during the performance. The three were all attending the concert separately, and even though they attended the same high school, they were not friends.

Brigette and Timothy had left the dance area of the concert at around 1:30 a.m. and went to a secluded park area on the concert grounds. At between 2:00 and 2:30 a.m., John and Kyle separated as Kyle needed to use the washroom and was going to look for "some tail."

John said that Kyle was out of sight for about twenty minutes, but other witnesses said he didn't return until 3:30 a.m. The witnesses said that when Kyle returned, he looked normal, no scratches or bruises on his face, and his clothes were clean, no dirt or mud on them. Kyle left the concert by car at 4:30 a.m.

Timothy returned from the woods without Brigette around 4:00 a.m. and his face and clothes were covered in mud, and he had scratches and blood on his face. Timothy claimed that he was in a fight with an unknown man, and he had passed out for a while after the fight was over.

Timothy stayed and partied with his friends at the concert until it was light outside. When he was leaving with a friend, he made his friend stop so that Timothy could light a fire in a barrel which was at the entrance of the concert grounds.

During the trial, evidence was brought out about blood found on Timothy's shoes that was consistent with Brigette's, as well as hair found on her body was that Timothy's. As well, Timothy left his pubic hairs on her body.

The evidence against Kyle was that police found a single hair from his scalp on Brigette's sweatshirt. Remember this was all done before DNA was used in court.

During the first interview between the police and Timothy, they noted the scars on his face and hands, and he admitted to having consensual sex with Brigette. He then told police that he had been attacked by an unknown man, who beat him and left him unconscious. Police also asked Timothy if he knew Kyle, and he said that he didn't. Detectives thought that it was possibly Kyle that attacked Timothy.

In Timothy's second interview, he now told police that Kyle killed Brigette and, in fact, made Timothy punch Brigette a few times and made him help move her body.

On the following day, Brigette's body was found in a creek in a park area of the concert grounds. She had been beaten severely, struck several times in the head, and strangled to death. There were also bite marks on her body, and a stick had been shoved up her vagina and anus.

Both Timothy and Kyle were charged with first-degree murder. Kyle's preliminary hearing resulted in a stay of proceedings. With only a single hair to tie Kyle to the murder, the detectives then interviewed at least twenty inmates that knew him, and five of them said that Kyle had talked about the murder of Brigette.

By the time court was held, only one of the five were found reliable enough to testify. But the defense was able to prove that the inmate had lied about the confession.

On June 13, 1991, the RCMP embarked on a Mr. Big operation against Kyle Unger. It started with two undercover policemen that pretended to have a broke-down car outside of the Hobby Farm in Manitoba, where Kyle lived. After getting some help with their car, the detectives befriended Kyle and started to use him in small illegal activities.

There were only four undercover detectives taking part in this Mr. Big sting, and it wasn't more than a month before Kyle met Mr. Big. Mr. Big told Kyle that he had heard that Kyle had whacked someone once, and that was excellent, as that's the kind of guys that he was looking for to be on his team.

It was then that Kyle admitted to the murder with pride. This then led to him getting arrested again for the murder of Brigette.

On February 22, 1992, both Timothy and Kyle were convicted of the first-degree murder of Brigette. The two men then appealed their convictions, with Kyle's being upheld, but Timothy was given a new trial. Timothy was released, but before he was retried, he committed suicide.

It wasn't until over ten years later, with the advent of DNA testing being used in court, that the single hair that was found on Brigette's body and thought to belong to Kyle was tested, and scientifically found not to be his.

On September 13, 2004, thirteen years after Kyle's original conviction, a new trial was finally granted. It took another four years before he was finally cleared on October 23, 2009, when the Manitoba Deputy Attorney General formally withdrew the charges against Kyle and asked for him to be acquitted. However, there would be no public enquiry or compensation offered for Kyle's wrongful conviction.

So, although the Manitoba Crown chose to withdraw the charges against Kyle, it was not willing to offer him any sort of compensation for the fourteen years that he ended up being in prison. In September 2011, Kyle filed a civil lawsuit seeking $14.5 million in damages.

Kyle Unger's case shows how easy it was to entice someone into a false confession, when it gives them the benefit of money, power and friendships. Some of the Mr. Big confessions also stem from violence and fear that's put onto the person being played by the undercover police.

ALAN SMITH 2009

'Change your thoughts and you change your world.' – Norman Vincent Peale

---

| Alan Smith

Alan Dale Smith was charged with first-degree murder in the 1974 death of 22-year-old Beverly Lynn Smith, who was not related to him, in her Oshawa,

Ontario home. Alan Smith had been Beverly Smith's neighbor and long-time suspect in her murder for decades, but they just didn't have any evidence to support a charge of murder.

It was on December 9, 1974, when Douglas Smith last saw his wife, when he left for work at the Oshawa General Motors plant at 7 p.m. where he worked the night shift. When he pulled out of his driveway, he looked in his rear-view mirror and saw his wife holding their baby girl and helping her wave bye to him.

The couple had been having a real struggle trying to take care of their 10-month-old baby girl, enough so that she left her job at the unemployment center so that she could focus full-time on their baby girl. Douglas would be sure to call her at home every night that he worked at least three times, just to check in, find out how she was doing and show his support.

It was on that December night that Douglas called her as usual but got no answer. After trying several times to call, he decided to call his neighbor Alan Smith and ask him if he would run over and check on his wife. Alan was busy working on fixing the water drain in their kitchen, so asked his wife to run over and check on Beverly.

It was only a matter of minutes when Alan's wife ran back into their house and yelled to Alan that Beverly was lying on the floor and needed help. He then called Doug at his job and told him that he needed to come home right away, as his wife was lying on the floor.

Beverly had been shot in the back of the head with a .22 caliber gun, and her baby was sleeping in the next room, seemingly unaware of what had happened. This was the first homicide for the Durham Regional Police force, which just happened to be formed that same year.

Their first suspect at the time was, of course, Beverly's husband, Douglas, to whom she had been married for four years. He was quickly ruled out by the police within two weeks, and the case eventually went cold. The murder always stayed on the minds of the police but was never actively investigated again until 1987.

Beverly's twin sister, Barbra Brown, made an emotional appeal for someone to come forward and help them find her sister's killer. The police received plenty of tips after Brown's press conference which reopened the case, and there were ten detectives put back on the case.

The only lead that the police had was that there was some marijuana missing from Beverly's home, so the murder might have been drug related. The detectives re-interviewed over 200 people and asked for voluntary DNA samples and fingerprints from each of them.

Police had always suspected that the murderer of Beverly was somebody that she knew. When the police arrived at the two-story rental house that Beverly had lived in, they found no sign of struggle. The Smith's dog was a loud and uncontrollable barker but hadn't made a sound that night, said other neighbors.

There were no unusual tire tracks or footprints found on the property. By all evidence Beverly had let her killer in the front door and even appeared to sit and talk with whoever it was. In Beverly's ashtray on her kitchen table, there was a smoldering cigarette and butt found.

Beverly was lying on her back; her feet were stretched under the kitchen table and blood had pooled around her head. The only thing that was found to be missing was three one-ounce bags of marijuana.

In March of 2008, the police arrested Alan Smith and charged him with second degree murder after his ex-wife, Linda, came forward with information that incriminated him.

Linda told the detectives that the murder weapon, the 22-caliber gun, was buried at the local humane society. That wasn't true. Linda then told detectives that she heard the shot when it happened. But later she changed her story, now saying that Alan was in the house with her when she heard the shot.

A few months later, in July, the Crown withdrew their charges against Alan Smith as they felt Linda, his ex-wife, had misled the detectives and kept changing her stories. Linda Smith would later plead guilty to obstruction of justice.

Linda Smith's attorney, Kevin Mitchell-Gill, said that she was carrying a lot of trauma and suffered from mental difficulties.

Alan Smith walked out of the courthouse with his family and thanked all his supporters during the terrible ordeal. But what Smith didn't know was that detectives were now focused on him as the only major suspect and had created a plan to get the evidence that was required to get him convicted for the murder. This time they would bring in the Mr. Big sting from the RCMP to get the evidence needed.

MR. BIG STING: PROJECT FEARLESS

It only took the Mr. Big sting about six months to get the confession that they needed to arrest Alan Smith for first degree murder. This was dubbed as "Project Fearless" and began in early 2009. Smith had been lured into his favorite sport, fishing.

Undercover detectives had told Smith that he had won a weekend fishing package and took him away. It was at this free fishing trip that Smith met another contest winner, who was really an undercover agent. This agent was posing as a broke loner who just got out of jail and was stuck living in his daughter's basement. By the end of the fishing trip, the two men were friends and had planned several other fishing trips. Over the next few months, the undercover agent and Smith went on several trips together and became quite close.

It wasn't long before the undercover officer started involving Smith in fake criminal behaviors such as small drug deals, where Smith would get paid for his help. This, of course, like all the other stings, would soon lead Smith to meeting the so- called Mr. Big. That's where they told Smith that they had a plan to rob a drug dealer of $80,000.

Smith was called later that same week and told there was a problem with the robbery, and they needed to see him right away. When Smith showed up to the industrial park where the robbery was supposed to take place, he found Mr. Big covered in fake blood and standing over what appeared to be a dead body.

It was just a mannequin wrapped in tarps and weighted down to feel like the weight of a body. Smith then helped Mr. Big burn the evidence at the scene and drop the fake body off a cliff. It was soon after this event that Mr. Big approached Smith and told him that he needed to know some incriminating information about Smith, as insurance that Smith wouldn't go to police about the murder.

Smith then gave the first of two confessions to Mr. Big, that he killed Beverly Smith alongside another man. The detectives were confused on who this other man would be, so they kept the sting going to find out any more information that they could.

It was about six months later when Smith came forward with a second confession to the murder of Beverly Smith, but this time he told them that he was alone. Smith was then arrested and charged with first degree murder. Smith would remain locked up for another four years before his trial was held.

The elaborate year-long sting would not hold up in Court. An Ontario Superior Court judge ruled that all the evidence gathered during the sting was inadmissible at trial. Justice Bruce Glass wrote that the police tactics had violated Smith's Charter of Rights, were an abuse of the process, and the sting had produced confessions so unreliable you could drive a Mack truck through all the holes. It was in Glass's opinion that the use of the information obtained in this manner would shock the sense of trial fairness to Canadian society.

Glass's dismissal of the sting evidence meant that Smith was a free man. The Crown lawyer, Paul Murray, said that there wasn't a likelihood of another trial. Smith walked out of the courthouse free for the first time in more than four years.

Alan Smith, now 66, told a Star reporter that "They put me through all kinds of horrific scare tactics. I thought my life was in jeopardy, is this what we do in this country?" Smith filed a $19 million lawsuit in January 2016 against a dozen officers from three different Ontario police agencies who ran the controversial operation against him.

Smith has also sued the Attorney General of Ontario and three Crown attorneys who counseled homicide investigators throughout their increasingly complex undercover operation. Smith alleges that the Crown knew, or should have known, the police tactic in the case created a risk of false confessions or wrongful imprisonment.

The police misused their power and breached their oath of office. The attorney and his agents misused and abused their offices, Smith alleges in his court papers.

6

DANIEL MORCOMBE MURDER

"Reality is easy. It's deception that's the hard work." – Lauryn Hill

---

| Brett Cowan

It was in 2003 when 13-year-old Daniel Morcombe of Queensland, Australia, went missing, and the police couldn't find a crime scene, a body or a potential murderer. They decided to try out the Mr. Big operation that had been successful in Canada for about ten years at the time.

Morcombe was abducted from a bus stop under the Kiel Mountain Road overpass in the sunshine coast of Australia on Sunday December 7, 2003. He left his home to go to the local mall to get his hair cut and to buy Christmas gifts for his family at about 1:30 in the afternoon, but he never returned.

Later witnesses reported to seeing Morcombe around 2:10 p.m. waiting for his bus under the Kiel Mountain Road overpass, but the bus that he was supposed to catch never arrived, as it had broken down a few miles before Morcombe's stop.

Shortly after, a replacement bus passed by the stop, and the driver reported seeing Morcombe and two other men waiting at the stop, but the driver went by them without picking them up due to the delays and radioed into the depot to have another bus sent out. When the other bus came along, Morcombe and the men were gone already.

Police canvassed the area, talked to any witnesses and reviewed all known child sexual felons known in the area, but the case went cold. It wasn't until May of 2009 when a full-size clay model of the man that witnesses had described was placed at the location where Morcombe had disappeared. Detectives were inundated with over 100 leads per day.

It only took another two months for an inquest to be held, where the court heard testimony from witnesses and several persons of interest. In Australia, there had been a law passed that the media could not report the names of people that are suspects or of interest to the police, as it could damage their reputations.

The police came up with a suspect by the name of Brett Peter Cowan because of his history of sexual assault on young boys. Cowan's first molestation occurred in December of 1987 when he was 18 years-old. He was charged for luring a 7-year-old boy into a park bathroom and molesting him and served three years in prison.

In 1993, only a year after Cowan was released from prison, he raped a 6-year-old boy outside of a different park, this time leaving the boy seriously injured and abandoned in a car in the bush. Cowan was caught and sentenced to 7 years for that crime, but only served four-and-a-half years.

Shortly after his release from prison, he moved to the Sunshine Coast and lived with his uncle and aunt. Cowan became a Christian and attended church regularly. He was married in 1999 and had a son before divorcing in 2004. Cowan became a suspect because of this history, as well as he was living close to where Morcombe went missing.

The detectives became focused on Cowan and were determined to put him away, but the evidence wasn't there, so they decided to try using the Canadian technique, otherwise known as the Mr. Big sting. While it was not the practice to use such a sophisticated and expensive operation in a missing persons case, the police thought it was necessary to catch Cowan.

It started on a flight heading to Perth, Australia, when Cowan met a man named Paul Fitzsimmons, also known as Fitzy. Fitzy was really an undercover policeman posing as a crime boss who gained Cowan's trust, and the two became friends. Over a period of several months, Fitzy's gang took Cowan through an array of small crimes such as drug deals and stealing cars.

The gang then offered Cowan a subpoena for his alibi in the Morcombe disappearance case, but Cowan denied any involvement in the case. It wasn't until August of 2011 when Cowan was at a hotel with some of Fitzy's' gang that he confessed his involvement in the abduction of Morcombe. The whole confession was caught on video tape.

Shortly after Cowan admitted to his involvement in Morcombe's disappearance, he led the undercover detectives to the remains of Morcombe's body. On August 21, 2011, two shoes and three human bones were found at the location Cowan took the undercover police to. Forensics later confirmed that they were the remains of Morcombe. It was then that the detectives arrested Cowan and charged him with the offences of murder, child stealing, deprivation of liberty, indecent treatment of a child under 16 years of age, and interfering with a corpse.

On February 7, 2013, Cowan stood trial at the Supreme Court of Queensland in the state capital of Brisbane. Cowan had a defense of only confessing to the murder and other crimes that were committed on Morcombe because of a lucrative money deal that was offered to him, and the fake gang had dangled a carrot in front of Cowan in the form of big money.

The prosecution presented their case which included 116 witnesses and over 200 exhibits. Cowan pled not guilty and declined to testify. On March 13, 2014, Cowan was found guilty of all charges and sentenced to life in prison with the possibility for parole after 20 years.

Cowan had undergone many psychiatric examinations since his first offenses in the late 1980s, and he was assessed with being a pathological liar with low-level psychopathic features or mild psychopathy, which is now known as antisocial personality disorder.

The appeals of the Cowan conviction have begun because of entrapment laws. The long arm of the Mr. Big technique is now under scrutiny in Australia since the Canadian Supreme Court ruling that limits its use in Canada due to the privacy infringements it puts on Canadians.

The first appeal was a positive result for the prosecution team, as the judgement allowed the confession made to the undercover police for the fact that Cowan led them to the remains of the victim, therefore bringing new evidence forward that confirmed the murder of Morcombe. This seems to be the only saving grace for the successful prosecution of people that have confessed to crimes during the Mr. Big operation.

7

OPERATION EZDELL

"The journey of a thousand miles begins with one step." - Lao Tzu

Rachel Nickell was living with her boyfriend, Andre Hanscombe, a motorcycle messenger, their 2-year-old son Alexander, and their dog, in the Wimbledon Common area of London, UK. On the morning of July 15,

1992, as Nickell and Alexander were walking their dog in their neighborhood, a man attacked her.

The attacker slit her throat with a knife and stabbed her forty-nine times before raping her, all while their son Alexander and their puppy watched. Later another person happened to be walking the same road and saw Alexander holding his mother's blood-soaked top and asking her to wake up.

This was a crime that shook the country and quickly made it a priority for the police. Police interviewed over 30 men in the Nickell murder, and the prime suspect became Colin Stagg, who was known to walk his dog in the same area regularly and was unemployed at the time.

OPERATION EZDELL

The Metropolitan Police Special Operations Group had an undercover female officer pretend to be a friend of a woman who used to talk with Stagg through a lonely-hearts column. The undercover introduced herself as Lizzie James, and she pretended to have a romantic interest in Stagg. She talked with him on the phone and mailed letters for about five months, and they eventually met in person.

There was a total of forty letters that Lizzie sent to Stagg over the five-month period, with each one of the letters getting more explicit. Lizzie was demanding that Stagg should confess to the murder of Nickell in return for him having sadomasochistic sex with her.

She told him that she wanted to be completely in his power, defenseless and humiliated, and even sent him a tape where she fantasized about a man holding a knife to her throat while having sex with her. Lizzie also told Stagg that it wouldn't matter to her if he did kill Nickell; in fact, it would be great if he had done it. It would have been a real turn-on to think about the man that did that. But even after that, Stagg insisted that he had nothing to do with it and that he could have just told her that he did to have sex with her.

So, with limited evidence collected by August of 1993, about six months into the operation, police decided to arrest Stagg for the murder of Nickell.

During the committal hearing, the justice ruled that the police had shown excessive zeal and had tried to incriminate a suspect by deceptive conduct of the grossest kind. He therefore excluded the Mr. Big Operation Ezdell, and the prosecution withdrew its case. Stagg was then acquitted in September of 1994.

Every year on the anniversary of the murder, Scotland Yard came under fire from the public to solve the case.

Scotland Yard responded by using a cold case review team, which used the latest in DNA techniques, reanalyzed witness statements, reviewed the files collected on possible suspects, and examined potential matches to other crimes for similarities and came up with nothing.

In July of 2003, police were able to further test Nickell's clothes, and police found a male DNA sample that did not match Nickell's boyfriend or son, and it ruled out the current list of suspects.

It was in July 2006, Scotland Yard decided to interview Robert Napper, who had been convicted of the murder of Samantha Bisset and her four-year-old daughter Jazmine in November 1993, about 16 months after Nickell's murder.

By November 2007, Napper was charged and

convicted of Nickell's murder. Eventually he pled guilty to manslaughter on the grounds of diminished responsibility. He was sentenced to the Broadmoor Hospital indefinitely as he was considered a very dangerous man.

Colin Stagg was then given a public apology from the police department. After the apology, Stagg sued the police department for damages of £1 million for the 14 months that he had to stay in prison. Stagg eventually received £760,000 in a settlement from the police.

The undercover police officer Lizzie James took an early retirement from the police force in 1998. She then sued the police department for damages arising from the undercover operation. The police settled for £125,000 in an out-of-court settlement, in which her lawyer stated, "The willingness of the Metropolitan Police to pay substantial damages must indicate their recognition that she sustained serious psychiatric injury."

There was an internal review of the Ezdell Operation where it was estimated that it cost about £3 million. Even with the severe criticism of Operation Ezdell, police mounted similar operations, called Century, as a part of their investigation of the Rettendon Triple Murders which proved to be unsuccessful as well.

OPERATION CENTURY – THE ESSEX BOYS

On the morning of December 7, 1995, farmers Peter Theobald and Ken Jiggins headed out to feed their animals in Rettendon, Essex. When they arrived at their farm, they found their gate entrance had been blocked by a Range Rover. The farmers stopped, and Ken approached the Range Rover's driver side window and knocked on it while asking him if he could move the Range Rover so that they could get into their farm.

After several knocks and no answer, Ken opened the front driver's side door and a male body slumped out towards him. Ken was startled and yelled out to Peter that the man was dead and there was blood all over the inside of the car. Peter came quickly to look in the car and saw that there were two other men in the car that had also been shot.

Tony Tucker, Patrick Tate, and Craig Rolfe had been shot in the head and left dead in their Range Rover.

The three men were part of a drug gang called the "Firm" and had been well known in the Essex community, as they had recently been suspected of selling some ecstasy pills to an 18-year-old girl named Leah Betts, who later died from the drugs. One of the three men had been a doorman at a nightclub where he would allow drug sales in the club.

It was later in December that police started their undercover sting operation called "Century" in which the detectives posed as an Irish Republican group which believed in the independence of Ireland from Great Britain. They called the two suspects of the Essex murders and told them that one of the men killed had owed them money and they wanted to collect off them.

After about five months of not getting any sort of evidence from the two suspects, the police decided to end the operation and try to convict the men with what evidence they did have. The two men, Jack Whomes and Michael Steele, were convicted of the murders on January 20, 1998. After a trial, they were sentenced to life imprisonment.

Details of the undercover operation became known during their trial in 1997, which included threatening phone calls to the suspects, who had recorded the calls for themselves as they didn't believe that the group was who they claimed they were.

The defense tried to use the "Ezdell Operation" case to show that "Operation Century" was also illegal practice, but the prosecution didn't use any evidence from the operation in court, and all their evidence came from after the operation had ended.

The courts in England described the tactics as disgraceful of the grossest kind. The convictions came because of a police investigation that happened after the Operation Century produced no evidence.

KLAUS FAMILY MURDER

> *"The essence of lying is in deception, not in words."* – John Ruskin

Jason Klaus

Recently, the details of a Mr. Big sting operation were used in the homicide case of the murders of three people in their Castor, Alberta, home on December 8, 2013. Jason Klaus was charged with three counts of first-degree murder and one count of arson for the deaths of his father Gordon Klaus, 61, his mother Sandra Klaus, 62, and his sister Monica Klaus, 40, and one count of endangering an animal for shooting and killing their family dog.

The remains of two of the Klaus family's bodies, Gordon and Monica, were found in their burned-down house in Castor, Alberta on December 3, 2013, whereas Sandra Klaus's body was never found. The police believe that she was consumed by the fire.

A second man, Joshua Frank, 32, was also charged with three counts of first-degree murder as Jason Klaus accused Frank of being the one that pulled the trigger on all three of the victims. According to Frank, Klaus didn't reveal that he was responsible for the murders of his own family until a couple of months after the deaths.

Frank claimed that Klaus had been doing some repo work but ended up getting into trouble with his boss for the murders. Frank said that Klaus told him that the boss was willing to help him out with an alibi. Klaus's boss said that he had an uncle that was dying of cancer and that his uncle would take responsibility for the murders and burning down the Klaus home.

For his dying uncle to make a confession to the crimes, he first would need to know the details of the crime. Jason then told Frank that he needed Frank to tell the story to his bosses to get him out of trouble with the boss, and if he didn't, there would be a bullet coming for him for sure. In Frank's mind, he had no choice but to take the rap for the crime even though he didn't want to.

Klaus then shared what story he wanted Frank to use on the bosses. He said that he just walked in and killed his mom and dad first, and then his sister in her room. He never said how many times he shot or any other details except that the family dog wouldn't stop barking, so he shot the dog, too.

Frank then asked Klaus why he did it, and Klaus replied that he was taken out of his parents' will, and everything was going to be left to his sister, Monica. Klaus had also forged over $6,000 in his dad's checks and he was worried that his dad was going to find out.

On August 16, 2014, Klaus made his confession to RCMP Staff Sergeant Mike McCauley in the Red Deer detachment. Klaus then admitted to coming up with the plan to murder his family with his friend Frank about one week before the murders happened.

Frank admitted to cashing about $5 or $6,000 in his dad's checks for some extra cash to take out some girls and maybe pay off a few bills he had, and his friend Josh Frank knew it. Klaus said when he told his friend about his problems with his dad's checks, Frank told him that he would take care of things. Klaus said that he didn't think it would happen and that he didn't really take Frank seriously.

Phone records showed that the two men had talked 28 times on the phone, and a few days before the murder, Klaus gave Frank his unregistered gun. In the police videotaped confession, Klaus said that he offered Frank about $20 or $25,000 eventually.

Despite admitting to his part in the crime, Klaus insisted that he was nowhere near the farm when his family was killed. Therefore, he wanted the charges on himself to be dropped. Klaus didn't realize that if you're part of the planning of a murder that you get charged with the murder whether you're there or not. Klaus then exclaimed that he was two miles down the road when the murders happened, and he had last-minute second thoughts. He was going to back out of the plan, but by then the farm was already on fire.

Frank had a different story of the murders and fire that night. Frank told the court that he was sitting in the passenger side of Jason Klaus's Suburban and the two of them were on their way to buy some cocaine, but Klaus drove them to his parents' farm and turned off the headlights and parked. Klaus then looked at Frank and told him not to make any noise, just sit there, and don't even think about leaving. Klaus got out of the vehicle and walked over to Frank on the passenger side and said, "If you want to make it through this night, you will shut the fuck up and do what I tell you."

Klaus then walked into the yard and around to the backside of the house. Shortly after, Frank said that he heard what he thought was loud voices. He then saw Klaus back on the driveway and saw a flash like a gunshot. Klaus then came back to the vehicle and opened Frank's door and told him to get out.

Klaus then told Frank to get into a white pick-up truck and start it up. While he was doing that, he saw Klaus go into a small shed and come out with a jerry can and go back into the house.

A few minutes later, Klaus came back out of the house and approached the white truck that Frank was warming up and told him to go back to his Suburban and follow him.

Klaus drove for about twenty minutes, then pulled over and approached Frank in the Suburban, gave him the keys to the white pick-up truck, and told Frank to throw the keys in a ditch somewhere. After Frank disposed of the keys, he got back into the Suburban with Klaus and they drove away.

It was a silent drive back to Castor until Frank asked Klaus what was going on. Klaus turned to Frank and told him to shut the fuck up, that he just lost his entire family and he didn't have time for his bullshit.

Klaus then pulled the vehicle over and told Frank to get out and warned him not to tell anybody or he would be fucking dead.

Frank also testified about the first time that he met Klaus was when he was 13. Frank was walking home from school where he had been beaten up earlier, and Klaus offered to give him a ride home. During that ride, Klaus offered Frank some cocaine. This was the first time that he had used cocaine and looked up to his new friend, even though Klaus was about six years older than Frank.

The next encounter was about a year later, when Klaus offered Frank a ride to work. During that ride, Frank claimed that Klaus sexually assaulted him. Frank then claimed their sexual relationship continued for about four more years until Frank was about 17. Frank said that he feared Klaus because of the years of rape and beatings and felt like he was owned by Klaus.

MR. BIG OPERATION

It was during the Mr. Big operation that Klaus admitted to the undercover detectives that he had hired Frank to commit the murders of his family because of his fear about his father finding out about the forged checks that he wrote.

Klaus also confessed that he had driven Frank to his

parents' farmhouse and waited down the road while Frank shot his family. Then they had taken his father's pick-up truck and abandoned it about 18 miles from the farm. It was also Frank that threw the murder weapon into the Battle River.

It should also be stated that Klaus gave the exact same confession to the police during his interrogation after he was arrested and charged. Klaus now knew that he was talking with people that he knew were police officers and still admitted to his involvement in the crimes.

When Frank met the undercover detectives in the Mr. Big Sting, he had given them the same story that Klaus had. In fact, after they both confessed to the Mr. Big undercover officers, they were very relieved that they were able to tell someone their story and felt that now they had gotten away with it, as the boss man was providing an alibi for them.

Now that the Supreme Court of Canada has placed strong barriers on the use of the Mr. Big operation, would this be yet another case where an appeal will overturn the conviction and allow for a second trial, only this time without the confessions derived from the sting?

One thing that swayed the Australian court to uphold their Mr. Big confession in the Daniel Morcombe murder was the fact that the suspect was able to lead the police to the body of the victim; therefore, the suspect brought new evidence to the investigation.

In this case, Frank told the police where he had thrown the murder weapon, and they were able to retrieve it. We will have to wait and see the outcome.

9

GARY JOHNSTON SURREY

"Success consists of going from failure to failure without loss of enthusiasm." – Winston Churchill

| Gary Johnston

It was in March of 1998 when Gary Johnston was robbing the Bridgeview home of one of his friends,

Jeanne Fraser. Vic Fraser, 43, Jeanne's brother, decided that he would drop by and see his sister as he finished work early that day. When he arrived at Jeanne's house, he startled Johnston, but he didn't realize that Johnston was robbing his sister's home, so he greeted him in a friendly manner. The two men had met before, and Fraser knew Johnston as one his sister's boyfriends.

Things quickly turned horrific as Johnston grabbed two knives from the kitchen and started stabbing Fraser into both sides of his neck. Johnston then grabbed Fraser's head and continued to stab his neck so hard that he broke both knife blades right into Fraser's neck. Fraser fell to the floor grasping for air but was still alive, so Johnston began kicking him all over his body.

Johnston, now panicking because Fraser was still alive, ran into the living room and grabbed a large shrub plant in a ceramic pot, carried it into the kitchen and smashed it onto Fraser's head. Finally, he stopped moving so Johnston then grabbed his wallet from his back pocket and left.

Johnston appeared on the police radar about eight months later. He was living in Regina, Saskatchewan when he was arrested and charged with second-degree murder for stabbing to death another man. He was later convicted and sentenced to 10 years in prison on April 10, 2000.

It was while Johnston was in prison that his brother, Michael, who had also been arrested for a different crime, told the detectives about the murder of Fraser that his brother had committed back in 1998. This information was given to the police to help get Michael's sentence reduced and therefore would not be strong enough evidence to get a conviction in court, so they didn't charge Johnston with the burglary or murder.

By August 2009, Johnston was released from prison on parole. He moved to Trenton, Ontario, and it was then that detectives decided to run the Mr. Big sting operation on Johnston over the Fraser murder.

MR. BIG OPERATION EPOLYGENOUS

The Mr. Big operation on Gary Johnston started in April of 2009, as they wanted to plan the details carefully. In August after Johnston was released from prison and moved to Trenton, a new neighbor was having a party to which he invited him.

Johnston had no way of knowing that the party was all undercover detectives pretending to be a group of criminals, so he felt at ease being there. It was the second get-together that Johnston was invited to that he met the fake kingpin or boss of the gang.

The Mr. Big operation continued for about six months total which included over 60 scenarios that enacted crimes in both Ontario and Quebec, paying out a total of $14,500 to win over Johnston's trust.

One of the scenarios set up by the undercover police was when they took Johnston to a cabin in the woods, where there were two kidnap victims bound with tape, and one of the operatives shot them three times to make it appear that they had been killed.

The fake gang boss asked to speak to Johnston alone at one of the parties, so they went into the bedroom. There the boss told Johnston that he was nervous about working with him because he had heard that some of Johnston's previous work was careless and sloppy. The boss had also heard that Johnston had told people about his crimes, including his own brother.

Johnston told the boss that he hadn't told anybody anything and had gotten much more careful after spending seven-and-a-half years in jail for a murder he committed in Regina. Johnston then told the boss that he would be a great asset for his crime family. Johnston finished by saying,

---

"I do what I'm told and get the job done. I've been there, done that, got 10 shirts and don't mind doing it again."

The undercover detective pretending to be the boss kept telling Johnston that his concern was DNA or fingerprints that could connect Johnston to the crime in Surrey and thought they were a loose end that he didn't want to see come back and haunt them.

After a few hours, Johnston stood up and demonstrated how he stabbed Fraser in the neck. He assured the boss that the police would never find the handles because he dumped them in various places and all they could possibly find was the pieces of knife blade that broke off into Fraser's throat. Johnston then told them that he burned all the clothes that he was wearing during the murder in a friend's fireplace.

The whole confession was videotaped. He was arrested and stood trial for the murder of Vic Fraser and was found guilty in November of 2011, sentenced to life and not eligible to apply for parole for 17 years.

APPEAL

In April of 2014, Johnston appealed his conviction arguing the trial judge erred in admitting a statement given by his brother, failing to exercise caution with considering evidence from an unsavory witness, and relying on a confession Johnston gave to undercover officer during a Mr. Big style-sting.

Three court of appeal justices disagreed, saying that the judge made no such errors. They dismissed the appeal on April 11, 2011.

SECOND APPEAL

Gary Johnston appealed to the Supreme Court of BC in 2015 on the basis that the elaborate five-month Mr. Big sting, despite the newer and tougher guidelines that were imposed by the Supreme Court of Canada in 2014, was an abuse of process because police made it appear that two people were kidnapped, beaten and then killed during the operation. Johnston also claimed that the police preyed on his poverty and loneliness upon release from prison after serving time for another murder.

In early 2016, the three justices on the appeal panel of the Supreme Court of BC disagreed with Johnston. Justice David Frankel wrote with the support of colleagues Daphne Smith and Edward Chiasson.

> "Although Mr. Johnston was unemployed, there is no suggestion he was destitute or socially isolated. The police neither preyed on his vulnerabilities, nor

directed violence or threats of violence at him or anyone close to him."

10

PROJECT KOLUMBO

Shawn Wruck

Stephanie Collins had reported her sister, Shannon Collins, 29, missing in September 2007. Stephanie had heard that her sister had left her legitimate job in Edmonton and went to Calgary to work for the Hell's Angels as a prostitute. She had left her 11-year-old boy behind.

The remains of Shannon Collins were found on June 5, 2008, in the Belvedere Heights area of Sherwood Park.

Shawn Wruck was found guilty of the second-degree murder of Shannon Collins in January of 2017.

Shawn Wruck had killed Shannon on December 22, 2007, after she had badmouthed him and began saying bad things about his sister, who had earlier killed herself.

MR. BIG STING PROJECT KOLUMBO

Shawn Wruck was tired of his job as a welder up in Fort McMurray and always dreamed of being a member of a crime organization. So, when he met a member of an undercover Mr. Big sting that were pretending to be a criminal organization, he got excited and was more than willing to join.

"Project Kolumbo" began in November 2012, when two undercover detectives moved into an apartment in Kelowna, B.C., next door to Wruck and his, at the time, live-in girlfriend. They worked their way into their new next-door neighbors' lives by inviting them over to birthday parties, for drinks at Christmas and more.

It was at these casual events that the male undercover detective would tell Wruck about the crime group that he had been a part of. It all seemed very natural that the two couples developed a good friendship.

Wruck was paranoid about being caught by the RCMP but was eager to meet the crime boss of the gang his neighbors were a part of, so that he could become a part of the gang. The undercover Mr. Big encouraged Wruck to get off the drugs he was using and to always be honest with him.

Wruck was now included in several trips to pick up and drop off cash or guns for the group and would get paid in cash for his work. Once he was even flown to Montreal for a UFC Championship for being part of an illegal drop of weapons.

The undercover detectives then invited Wruck to a retirement party for one of their gang members at a men's club so that he could see that it was okay to leave the gang at any time. That night, the gang made it clear that they would protect him if he was honest about any crimes that he had committed in the past. Wruck then spoke about murdering Collins.

A short time later, one of the undercover officers pretended he was in trouble with a woman who was trying to extort him. In a staged abduction, the gang took the woman out into the bush and put a gun into her mouth to scare her, then let her go. Wruck was frightened by this, and he told the gang again about killing Collins.

In the following spring, Wruck finally got a meeting with Mr. Big in an Edmonton industrial park, where he eventually told Mr. Big in detail how he had killed Collins. During the confession, Wruck also gave a re-enactment of the murder and showed them where he dumped the body of Collins.

Mr. Big then asked Wruck for the Rubbermaid container that he had kept Collins's body in for several days until he dumped it. Wruck seemed to become irritated by the request, and he told the undercover officer that he would get it for him later.

After Wruck got back to his Kelowna apartment, he started to get scared that he might have been tricked, so he started to send texts to the gang members denying that he had any involvement in the murder of Collins.

> "Dude, I don't have that thing. I never did,"

was the first text.

> "I didn't do what I told you and your uncle. I was just trying to impress you guys cause that's what you wanted to hear,"

Wruck said in his next text.

> "I'm sorry for deceiving you. But, if I was to do that kinda thing, I sure as fuck would never tell anyone, I'm sorry. Please don't hold this against me bro. I'm pretty sure I know who did it. But, just made shit up to look like a heavy hitter. I never did that thing, I swear. I wasn't scared to admit it because I'm innocent,"

Wruck said in his next text.

Even after Wruck sent the texts telling the gang that he had just lied about murdering Collins, he was arrested and charged with the first-degree murder of Collins.

Before the case could go to trial, the court had to decide on whether the Mr. Big operation details would be allowed into evidence.

In June 2016, the court ruled that the evidence could be

used even though it noted that it couldn't be sure that the confession was truthful.

The court heard the original tape of Wruck's confession to Mr. Big about killing Shannon Collins. On the tape, Wruck said that after Collins had badmouthed his sister, who had killed herself, he just snapped, and the next thing he knew he was on top of her and choked the wind out of her.

In January 2017, Shawn Wruck was found guilty of the second-degree murder of Shannon Collins, even though he was charged with first-degree murder, because the judge felt that the Crown was not able to prove any prior planning. In March 2017, Wruck was sentenced to life in prison with no chance for parole for 13 years.

11

DEREK KEMBEL MURDER CASE

| Christopher Shewchuk

Derek Kembel disappeared after leaving a bar in Dauphin, Manitoba on the evening of February 28, 2003. Kembel was at the Dauphin bar drinking and listening to music when a woman across the room started to flirt with him. He ended up buying the woman a drink and walked over to talk with her.

The couple really hit it off and were so focused on each other that they didn't notice Christopher Shewchuk walk right up beside them until he threw his beer into the woman's face. Shewchuk was the lady's boyfriend, who then started calling the woman names and told her that it was over. The couple then got into a physical altercation until the bar's security came over and separated the couple, then threw Shewchuk out of the bar for the rest of the night.

The evening continued with Kembel and the lady staying at the bar for a couple more hours before they left for the girl's home. When they arrived at her house, Shewchuk was in the living room waiting for her. The three argued some more, then had some drinks before the girl passed out. Shewchuk then offered Kembel a ride home.

It was during the ride home that Shewchuk tells police that his truck broke down, and Kembel decided to walk home, and that was the last he saw him. Police questioned Shewchuk about Kembel but were unable to arrest him as there was no evidence, not even a body, available.

Police became suspicious when Shewchuk left town a few days later, then when he returned, he had a brand-new interior in his truck.

MR. BIG STING

It was almost eleven years later that the RCMP decided to try solving the Kembel missing persons case with a Mr. Big operation. It started when an undercover agent approached Shewchuk in a bar in Dauphin, Manitoba, by asking him for help to track down a person who had wronged the gang.

The operation lasted about four months and included fifty-eight different scenarios with Shewchuk in hopes to gain his trust enough for him to confess to the crime. It started out with jobs for him to pick up and drop off bags of guns or drugs, and he got paid cash for each.

Shewchuk got so involved in the criminal activity that he started to offer to kill anybody for the gang.

Slowly the story was coming out about his relationship with Kembel. He had first told the undercover detectives that he saw his girlfriend flirting with Kembel when they were all at a bar together. A fight ensued and Shewchuk broke up with her right at the bar, and he left the bar shouting at the couple.

Later that night, Kembel got invited to the girl's apartment to continue drinking, but when they arrived they found Shewchuk there waiting. The three of them had some more drinks before the girl passed out, then Shewchuk offered Kembel a ride home.

On the drive to Kembel's home, words were exchanged, and Shewchuk pulled over, grabbed a shotgun that he always carried in his truck, and shot Kembel. Shewchuk then took Kembel to his farm and burned the body and scattered his remains in a field close to his farm.

Eventually Shewchuk even took some of the undercover gang members to the place where he left the pieces of the burnt remains.

"I fucking blasted him with a shotgun, I put a bullet right through him. Right through his fucking chest,"

Shewchuk said on tape. He then calmly said,

> "I then fired a second shot right through his skull, then burned his body, made sure there were no bones, no teeth, nothing, there'll be no pieces of the body left."

The undercover police officer that he was speaking to at the time was pretending to be a hit man. He confessed while the two men were on a trip to Montreal in January 2011. When Shewchuk was asked if he regretted doing the killing or it kept him awake at night, he responded by saying,

> "I felt more guilt killing a deer."

Shewchuk was arrested and charged with first-degree murder for the death of Derek Kembel in 2011. Police also charged Thomas Shewchuk with accessory after the fact murder, but they did not explain why or the relationship between the two Shewchuk men.

On March 1, 2003, Shewchuk, 32, pled guilty to the second-degree murder for the fatal shooting death of Derek Kembel, 25. Kembel's body was never recovered, just a few bone fragments and his watch. Shewchuk's admission of guilt came just before the first-degree murder trial was set to begin.

Shewchuk automatically received a sentence of life behind bars without a chance of parole for 10 years, but the prosecutors got his parole eligibility set at 13 years.

ANDREW ROSE

Andrew Rose

In August 1983, two young German tourists, Bernd Goericke and his fiancée, Andrea Scherp, went on a hiking trip through western Canada in the region known as the Kootenays. The trip was a wedding gift from their families in Germany. It was during this trip that the two of them would be found shot to death on a remote trail about 30 kilometers from the town of Chetwynd, British Columbia.

Both victims had been shot in the head, and their passports, money, and travelers checks were missing from the scene, so robbery was the suggested motive.

The RCMP spent months canvassing the local residences and searching the land for clues. The only piece of physical evidence they found was a size 34 waist pair of blue jeans that were covered in blood, about one mile from the bodies. The blood was tested, and it matched the two German tourists and one unknown person. Six years passed with nothing new, and the case went cold.

In 1989, there was a finally a break in the case, when a drug dealer, who was also a police confidential informant, told the detectives about a woman who claimed she knew who committed the murders. This led police to a woman named Madonna Kelly, who told them that a friend of hers, Andy Rose, showed up at her trailer the night of the murders in 1983, and he was covered in blood all over his face and clothes. Rose then told Madonna about killing two German tourists that night.

The police decided to put a wire on Rose's phone and asked Madonna to call Rose and talk to him about when he came to her trailer that night, and about the murders. After a few calls between the two, and still no confession, police decided to arrest Andy Rose for the murder of the two German tourists.

Even though Rose did wear size 34 jeans, the testing of the blood at the time was unable to link him to the jeans. The German's traveler's checks were cashed later hundreds of miles away from the murder site and by two men, neither of whom matched Rose's description. The primary piece of evidence was the testimony by Madonna Kelly.

Rose was then convicted of two counts of first-degree murder in 1991. Rose appealed the case and it was overturned because the appeals court found sufficient circumstantial evidence to create doubt, and he was granted a new trial.

During the next twelve years, Andy Rose had a second trial, with Madonna being the key witness. The second trial ended in a guilty verdict against Rose just as in the first trial, solely based on Madonna's testimony. Later that year, this conviction was overturned as well on a technicality. This left the police even more determined to get Rose put away for the murders. Now the RCMP decided to start a Mr. Big sting operation against Rose.

MR. BIG STING

Rose was released from prison and, having the past twelve years being in and out of jail and in court, he had no work history and couldn't find a job. So, when a man offered him a cash job running errands for him, Rose jumped at it.

The man that hired him was a supposed gang member but was really an undercover detective that was running a Mr. Big operation on Rose, to try and get a confession about the tourists' murders.

The undercover detectives tried saying anything they could to try and get the confession, even promising that they could take care of covering up the murders. But they were not able to get the confession.

During the Mr. Big operation, Rose was under great pressure to confess to the murder by the undercover detectives calling him names, swearing, threats and even challenges, but he maintained his innocence. Here is an example of an interview between Rose and Mr. Big:

> Mr. Big: That's a lie, that's a fuckin' lie right off the bat. Cuz everything I fuckin' found out about it, the evidence is all fuckin' there that you did it. They convicted you twice on the fuckin' thing, they can convict you a third time. Listen, I don't give a fuck.
>
> Rose: I do not lie to you.
>
> Mr. Big: I don't give a fuck, let's get that clear. But if you're just gonna lie to me, and you don't want fuckin' help, then I can't help you. I'm helping you because....
>
> Rose: If I tell you I didn't do it and you don't believe I didn't do it, what am I supposed to say? I need your help.
>
> Mr. Big: Yeah, well, you're not gonna fuckin' get it unless I get the fuckin' story. And I'll explain to you how...
>
> Rose: I didn't do it.
>
> Mr. Big: I'll explain to you how I can fuckin' help you.
>
> Rose: What can I say now?
>
> Mr. Big: Tell me the truth.
>
> Rose: I didn't do it.
>
> Mr. Big: Come clean with me and I'll tell you how I'm gonna help you.
>
> Rose: I didn't do it.
>
> Mr. Big: Well then you don't need my help.
>
> Rose: I'll never say I did it. I'll never say I did it, cuz I didn't.

Mr. Big: Well...

Rose: So, what can I say?

Mr. Big: Well, if you didn't do it, you don't need my help. Let's let the fuckin' courts decide. If I fuckin' help you out, you'd be guaranteed not to be found guilty, but I'm not fuckin' helping you out for the fuckin' uh, I don't fuckin'...

Rose: Yeah, but you want me to say I'm guilty.

Mr. Big: I want the fuckin' uh, I want to be able to fuckin' trust you. When I leave this fuckin' room, I know I've got a guy I fuckin' trust.

Rose: I know.

Mr. Big: All the fuckin' circumstances I have found out and I've looked into I have fuckin' come away fuckin' saying "Okay, this guy offs these two people, I don't give a fuck why. That's the least of my fuckin' worries. I will help him if he fuckin' just comes clean, and if he doesn't, then I'm not givin' him a fuckin' minute of my fuckin' time anymore."

Rose: I didn't do it, okay?

Mr. Big: Well then, there you go. You don't need my fuckin' help, do you?

Rose: Damn right I do.

Mr. Big: You better come clean.

Rose: Well I'm still not gonna say I did it cuz I didn't. So, what am I supposed to say?

Mr. Rose: From what I know, you haven't got a chance. That lady from the states, she'll not be givin' the evidence you think she's gonna be givin'.

Rose: No?

Mr. Big: The police have been fuckin' softshoein' her big time. That's why this has been fuckin' delayed the way it is.

Rose: I'll tell you right now, if this means the end of me and you and whatever, I will not say I did it. That's it. Then I'm outta here, you know, simple as that. That's the way she goes. I will not say I did it when I didn't do it, and I didn't do it and that's it.

Mr. Big: Go downstairs to the lounge, have one fuckin' beer, think this over.

Rose: Well, I'm not gonna come back up here and say I killed them.

Rose and another undercover detective went downstairs to a bar where they spent about two hours drinking beer. After they returned upstairs to the hotel room where Mr. Big had been waiting, Rose took a seat in the room across from him. Rose appeared quite intoxicated by this time and seemed to be real shaky and said,

---

"Well, we'll go with I did it, okay? Maybe I blacked out, you know."

Rose attempted to give details about the murder but did not know any of the details and would keep guessing wrong during his confessions. He didn't have any of the details in the case, didn't know if the tourists had been killed with a gun or rifle, or that their bodies had been moved.

After they got a couple of confessions by Rose on videotape, they went ahead and arrested him for the murders and started the process of a third trial against him for two counts of first-degree murder.

After retesting the jeans that were found at the crime scene for DNA, they found three blood types, which were the two German tourists and one other person, but it didn't match Rose. The Crown also had a logistical problem: when Madonna testified that Rose showed up to her trailer, which was about 20 miles from the murder scene, he was wearing those bloody jeans. So why would Rose travel over 20 miles to take those bloody jeans back to the crime scene and leave them there? Another issue was that Rose didn't have a car.

Andy also said that he was at a bar that night and was beat up by another patron at the bar, and that's why he had blood on him when he showed up at Madonna's trailer.

Another issue was when the police were able to trace the travelers checks that were taken from the murdered German tourists, being cashed hundreds of miles away from the crime scene, two males were described by witnesses, and neither of them looked like Rose.

The Crown decided to withdraw the charges against Rose. The prosecutor said that he did not feel comfortable going ahead with the trial because if he got the conviction, he wouldn't feel right. If a police officer offers some sort of thing to admit to a crime, it would not be admissible in court. Now if the person offering someone something for an admission wasn't a police detective, then it would be allowed into court.

INNOCENCE PROJECT

> *"If you want to conquer fear, don't sit home and think about it. Go out and get busy."* – Dale Carnegie

Three Innocence Projects have now taken up the case of West Vancouver men Atif Rafay and Sebastian Burns, who in 2004 were convicted of the 1994 slayings of Rafay's parents and sister in their Bellevue, Washington, home.

Former Vancouver teacher and writer, Ken Klonsky, is director of Innocence International, founded by the late Rubin "Hurricane" Carter in 2004. He decided to take on the case after seeing a film about the case made by Burns's sister. "It appeared very similar, the occurrences around both convictions had glaring similarities," he told On the Coast host Stephen Quinn, referring to an earlier exoneration he was part of, the case of David McCallum. He spent

29 years in prison before he was exonerated for a carjacking murder he didn't commit.

Klonsky believes that there's not enough evidence to convict Rafay and Burns and that the confession central to their 2004 conviction should be thrown out because it was a Mr. Big operation.

> "There was no hard evidence, or forensic evidence, tying the defendants to the actual crime."

For any Innocence Project, that's number one on the list. Second, there were false confessions, brought about through actual or implied brutality So they were ready to say anything to satisfy these 'gangsters'.

Klonsky says there was also evidence leading to other suspects that was not followed up on, and investigators developed tunnel vision on Rafay and Burns.

> "The problem with Atif and Sebastian back then was they were intellectuals, and there's a prejudice in society against young intellectuals. I think the police felt like, 'these guys aren't going to outsmart us. We're going to get 'em.' And that's why the RCMP was so willing to pick up the case when they came to Canada."

Klonsky said he is confident of the pair's innocence.

> "There are maybe 65 or 70 Innocence Projects in the United States. Two of them took up Sebastian and Atif's case before we did,"

he said, mentioning the University of Washington's Innocence Project Northwest and the Idaho Innocence Project. He says one of the challenges any new trial or acquittal of Rafay and Burns faces is unearthing all the evidence and having it tested.

Atif Rafay, a target of the controversial "Mr. Big" technique and one of Canada's most famous convicted killers, has said that he felt "extremely" threatened during the undercover operation meant to extract a confession of murder.

In an exclusive interview from prison, his first since his conviction in 2004, Rafay attacks the Mr. Big process, saying it

> "essentially makes you try to be as plausible as you can in your false confession, and that plausibility is what convinces a juror or someone else that 'Oh, it must be true despite all the countervailing evidence.'"

Rafay told the CBC's *The Fifth Estate* that he is hoping to have his case reopened, based on the Supreme Court ruling, though that seems unlikely, given that previous appeals in the U.S. to overturn his and Sebastian Burns's convictions, because much of the evidence against them was obtained by such a sting, have been unsuccessful. He spoke to *The Fifth Estate's* Bob McKeown from the Monroe Correctional Center outside Seattle, Washington.

Rafay and his friend Sebastian Burns were sentenced to 99 years in jail for the 1994 murder of Rafay's parents and sister at their home in Bellevue, Washington. The family had recently relocated from Vancouver while Rafay completed his freshman year at Cornell University in Ithaca, New York.

The jury at the men's six-month trial was told Rafay was motivated by money and planned the killings while Burns carried them out. The two men have spent nearly half their lives in prison serving three consecutive life sentences with no chance of parole. Illegal in most countries, including the U.S., the Mr. Big tactic had new limits imposed on it last summer by the Supreme Court, which said the operation risked producing unreliable confessions, but did not forbid it outright.

NEW LIMITS FOR 'MR. BIG' STING CONFESSIONS BY SUPREME COURT

In this kind of operation, police get murder suspects to confess by posing as a criminal gang and introducing suspects to a fake crime boss, Mr. Big, who says he can help them but only if they can prove their bona fides, usually by coughing up information about the crime they had been charged with.

In 2014, the Supreme Court ruling called into question the reliability of confessions obtained during such a sting, and legal experts say dozens of cases of convictions could come under review. Al Haslett was one of the originators of the technique in the early 1990s. Recently retired from the RCMP, he can now talk about his many cases as Mr. Big, coaxing confessions from murder suspects such as Rafay and Burns.

During the operation, Haslett asked Rafay how it felt to

> "kill your parents and knock off your sister?"

Rafay claimed that they did it for the family's insurance money, saying he felt,

> "pretty rotten, but it's tempered by the fact that I felt it was necessary to achieve what I wanted to achieve in this life. I didn't approve of the thing."

Rafay says he was angry when he learned Burns had got him involved with the supposed crime gang that was to somehow influence their case.

> "I mean, I didn't approve of the thing at all from the beginning. It seemed like nothing that I wanted to have much to do with."

He claims they never intended to do anything violent

for the crime boss, but they were willing to say whatever was necessary to get his help.

"I didn't want to become a hit man for him. I wanted to indicate to them that this is not something that I'm ever going to do, and yet at the same time, I'm not ever going to rat you out, I'm not going to do anything to compromise your organization."

Haslett is asked whether he believes Rafay and Burns could have felt threatened into making their confessions. Of Burns, Haslett says,

---

"I would never have said I'm ever going to do him any physical harm. If he had that perception, that is something that his imagination could've worked."

Asked if he did, indeed, feel threatened, Rafay said,

"Yeah, actually, extremely so. Really, it was all a dream world created out of movies. It would seem very possible after watching Goodfellas that Mr. Big would simply kill me because I was potentially a threat to him. That seemed completely convincing – in a way that would only be convincing to an 18-year-old kid."

Defense counsel Marie Henein argues in *The Fifth Estate* piece that threats of one kind or another are the very essence of the Mr. Big sting.

> "When you say it's imagination, they're not making it up. It's because they're told, 'You know who you're sitting with? You're sitting with somebody that kills people. So you might want to play ball.'"

14

PROJECT SOUVENIR

"The only thing we have to fear is fear itself." –
Franklin D. Roosevelt

| John Nuttall and Amanda Korody

A retired RCMP police detective, Alan Haslett, who helped develop and start the Mr. Big Sting operation, slammed the tactics publicly in July 2016 after doing the investigation of John Nuttall and Amanda Korody.

It was in 2015 when John Nuttall and Amanda Korody, a common-law couple, were convicted of conspiring to murder persons unknown and making or possessing explosive substance for a terrorist group as well as placing the explosive in a public place.

When the verdict was read out loud in court, Nuttall made a heart shape with his fingers and pointed it towards Korody. They were both facing life in prison.

The plan was to place a bomb in the parliament building in Victoria, British Columbia's capitol, during the legislative assembly and, therefore, committing murder. The conviction was put on hold while the defense argued that their clients were entrapped by the police during the Mr. Big operation against them.

The defense also argued that the police themselves were involved in as well as committed the same crimes that their clients did. The police manufactured this crime and that is not permitted in our law.

The police also gave spiritual advice to Nuttall and Korody that encouraged them to commit crimes.

The couple were arrested on July 1, 2013, the day they were accused of planting three pressure cooker bombs on the ground floor of the legislature.

The couple were described as poor, methadone-dependent former drug addicts who were radicalized by Islam to kill innocent people.

MR BIG OPERATION CALLED PROJECT SOUVENIR

The sting started on February 23, 2013, with an undercover RCMP officer that posed as an Arab businessman who made eye contact with Nuttall in a corner store close to Nuttall's home. A couple of days later, the fake Arab approached Nuttall to ask him if he would help to find the Arab's lost niece. It was during their time together talking about the lost niece that Nuttall told the Arab that he desired to wage a holy war on behalf of Islam.

The Arab then asked Nuttall if he would deliver a package, without knowing what was inside of it, to a locker inside the Vancouver bus terminal. It was to see if Nuttall was trustworthy as well as able to follow instructions.

In May the undercover detective then drove Nuttall and Korody to Whistler, B.C., so that Nuttall could drop off a hard drive that had plans to hijack a Via Rail passenger train, to another undercover officer that was posing as a terrorist.

The plan was not well researched by Nuttall, as the rail line had stopped operating the previous year. The undercover detectives yelled at him for creating such a bad plan. The couple then went to Victoria and took a guided tour of the legislature so they could figure out which symbols that they wanted to destroy. They then toured the Canadian Forces Base in Esquimalt as another place to conduct a possible attack.

The next contact was when the undercover police rented a hotel room in Kelowna, B.C. for three days in June of 2013, so that the couple could have a private place to work out their terrorist plot. It would also give the police access to the couple's basement suite apartment with them being away from town.

But the couple came back after their three-day holiday in Kelowna without a plan. The undercover detectives verbally attacked them, telling them that they showed a great deal of disrespect by not doing the work.

On June 29, Nuttall and Korody met with an undercover detective who posed as a terrorist, where they tried to get him to give them some C4 plastic explosive so that they could use it in their pressure cooker bombs.

The couple also made a video in which they were dressed in head scarves where they outlined the reasons that they were waging a war on non-believers, which was to be released after they committed a bomb attack.

On July 1, 2013, Nuttall and Korody took three homemade pressure-cooker bombs in a sports bag and hid it under some bushes outside of the B.C. Legislature. At about 4 a.m., they went back to their hotel in Vancouver and watched the news, waiting for the announcement of the bombing. They waited until about 2 p.m. the next afternoon before they left to go home. It was then that the police arrested them.

Documents later released show the RCMP paid more than 200 people, mainly police officers, $911,090.54 for overtime work during the Mr. Big investigation on the couple. The operation involved more than 240 police officers, most of them behind the scenes.

In a *Vancouver Sun* interview held on July 30, 2016, by Stephanie Ip, Retired RCMP Al Haslett said that the police that were engaged in this investigation never had the experience to be running something of this nature. They were not experts in undercover work, and they were out of their league. Haslett said,

---

"Mr. Big stings are very, very valuable and a

powerful investigative tool, and when they're run by the experienced experts in that field, they are run very smoothly; and they can either gather the proper evidence to take someone to court and get convictions or quite possibly gather evidence or gather facts that show the investigator these people are in fact not guilty, and what's what they could have done in the case."

Haslett continued his slam on the investigative team for not stopping the sting earlier, noting that an operation of this size would have required weekly, if not daily, reports up the chain of command, extending to Ottawa. Haslett stated,

---

"It's everybody, all the way up the ladder, who I really feel was out of their league in this investigation. Once it was determined that these two individuals can do this crime without totally being led around by the nose by the undercover operators, who were, in fact, RCMP, that right there should have set off signals that we are overstepping our boundaries here.

We are potentially putting this whole undercover technique at risk in front of our Canadian Courts. Mr. Big stings that are done on homicides and crimes of that nature are run by people who are experts and know what they're doing. There's only a handful of people in British Columbia that have the expertise to run a proper undercover operation, to be sure that all the checks and balances are in place, and there's a small amount across Canada.

I'm not surprised by the ruling of the judge, but when I think it through, I'm surprised the RCMP let this go on for as long as it did and how it did."

EPILOGUE

"There are things to confess that enrich the world, and things that need not be said." – Joni Mitchell

---

At the time of writing this book, the Crown has filed an appeal of the court throwing out the conviction of John Nuttall and Amanda Korody for their plot to explode three homemade bombs on the floor of the Victoria legislature.

The couple were found guilty in June 2015 of conspiring to commit murder, possessing an explosive substance and placing an explosive in a public place. Those convictions were put on hold for one year, until the appeals court decided that the couple had been entrapped by the police. The police were accused of using trickery, deceit, and veiled threats to engineer the bomb plot.

The prosecution said in court papers filed that Nuttall and Korody were completely responsible for crafting and carrying out the plan, and the undercover RCMP operation did not qualify as either manipulative or an abuse of power.

An average Canadian that was in the same position as this couple were, would not have done the things that they did. It was also the impression that, in the couple's mind, the explosion would be an act of jihad to strike terror in the hearts of Canadian infidels.

What will happen in this, like many of the other cases that have used the Mr. Big Sting, is yet to be seen. It seems that the appeals court in general has been staying convictions that have used this technique because it's a form of entrapment.

But when the court takes that opinion, though it does help those wrongly convicted such as displayed earlier in this book, it also appears to help couples like Nuttall and Korody, who went as far as actually planting the bombs with designs of hurting others.

ACKNOWLEDGMENTS

Thank you to my editor, proofreaders, and to the cover artist for your support! Also, I must thank my family at home as well as my family on the radio, you take me up!

ABOUT THE AUTHOR

Alan R Warren is one of the current hosts of the House of Mystery Radio Show that is heard on KKNW 1150 AM in Seattle and is syndicated in Utah on KVFX 98.3 FM and KYAH 540 AM in Salt Lake City and KFNX 1100 AM Phoenix. He has written three best selling True Crime books and articles for True Crime Case Files Magazine and Serial Killer Magazine.

Alan achieved his Masters in Music at the University of Washington and his minor in Criminology. He also has his recording and sound engineering certificate from the Award-Winning Bullfrog Studios in Vancouver B.C., Canada.

ALSO BY ALAN R. WARREN

BEYOND SUSPICION: RUSSELL WILLIAMS - A CANADIAN SERIAL KILLER

Young girl's panties started to go missing; sexual assaults began to occur, and then female bodies were found! Soon this quiet town of Tweed, Ontario, was in panic. What's even more shocking was when an upstanding resident stood accused of the assaults. This was not just any man, but a pillar of the community; a decorated military pilot who had flown Canadian Forces VIP aircraft for dignitaries such as the Queen of England, Prince Philip, the Governor General and Prime Minister of Canada.

This is the story of serial killer Russell Williams, the elite pilot of Canada's Air Force One, and the innocent victims he murdered. Unlike other serial killers, Williams seemed very unaffected about his crimes and leading two different lives.

Alan R. Warren describes the secret life including the abductions, rape and murders that were unleashed on an unsuspecting community. Included are letters written to the victims by Williams and descriptions of the assaults and rapes as seen on videos and photos taken by Williams during the attacks.

This updated version also contains the full brilliant police interrogation of Williams and his confession. Also the twisted way the Williams planned to pin his crimes on his unsuspecting neighbor.

DEADLY BETRAYAL : TRUE STORY OF JENNIFER PAN DAUGHTER FROM HELL

A family of three tied up, each with a gun to their head, "Where's the money? Where's the fucking money?" one of the intruders yelled. A petrified daughter tortured and forced to listen to her parents being shot in cold blood. "I heard shots, like pops," she told the 911 operator, "somebody's broke into our home, please, I need help!" Was this a home invasion? Or something else, more sinister, a deadly betrayal.

The real-life horror story that happened inside the Pan family home shocked their normally peaceful upscale Toronto neighborhood. The Pans were an example of an immigrant family. Hann and his wife, Bich Pan, fled from Vietnam to Canada after the U.S.-Vietnamese war to find a better life. Their daughter, Jennifer, was an Olympic-caliber figure skater, an award-winning pianist, and a straight A student.

The Pans worked their way up in this rags-to-riches story, now living in a beautiful home with luxury cars in the driveway. Was it these expensive items that lured three intruders with guns into their home on the night of November 8, 2010?

Find out what really happened when seasoned true crime

reporter and author, Alan R. Warren, takes you through the details as they unfold in this book of a deadly betrayal.

REFERENCES

1. Channel 4 Dispatch Program, 1994.
2. KIRO 7 News: *48 Hours Mystery Unravels Bellevue Murder Case*, Kirotv.com, 2007-09-13.
3. The Fifth Estate: *True Confessions - Timeline of Events*, Aired October 14, 2011.
4. CTV News: *Filmmaker explores issue of coerced confessions*, August 26, 2007.
5. Reid, Michael D.: *I'm tired of being quiet*, canada.com, February 4, 2008.
6. Baron, Ethan: *Innocent? Or guilty?*, The Province, November 5, 2008.
7. CBC News: *Vancouver men on trial for triple murder*, November 24, 2003.
8. Stasi, Linda: *Friends for Life*, New York Post, September 15, 2007.
9. Hutchinson, Brian: *Parents of a triple murderer vow to fight: 'We should have screamed out loud'*, National Post

10. CBC News: *B.C. men sentenced to life for triple murder*, October 23, 2004.
11. Seyd, Jane: *Killer's sister looks at 'Mr. Big' confessions*, Vancouver Courier, August 29, 2007.
12. R. v. Hart, scc-csc.lexum.com, July 31, 2014.
13. *Current Appeal Status*, Rafayburnsappeal.com.
14. Crime Watch, *Essex boy*, 1996.
15. Bernard O Mahoney

www.ingramcontent.com/pod-product-compliance
Lightning Source LLC
Chambersburg PA
CBHW011131070526
44583CB00023B/2985